13 Art Mysteries
Children Should Know

Angela Wenzel

PRESTEL

Munich · London · New York

Contents

This book will introduce you to thirteen art mysteries, all with one thing in common: None has been solved, despite the best efforts of scholars, artists, and amateur sleuths to get to the bottom of them. Here you can set out on their trail yourself. A timeline helps you place each mystery in its historical context. A glossary at the end of the book explains difficult terms, which are marked with an asterisk*. If you want to read more about these mysteries, we give you recommendations for interesting books and Internet sites. And finally, there are quiz questions and tips for experiments that you can do yourself!

Technical terms are explained here

1200s B.C. Exodus of the Israelites from Egypt ✳

ca. 1000 B.C. the Ark of the Covenant may have arrived in Jerusalem ✳

1500 B.C. 1450 B.C. 1400 B.C. 1350 B.C. 1300 B.C. 1250 B.C. 1200 B.C. 1150 B.C. 1100 B.C. 1050 B.C. 1000 B.C. 950 B.C.

Mystery:
  Where is the Ark of the Covenant?
Artist of the Ark:
  Unkonown
Date:
  The time of Moses
Location:
  Israel
Distinguishing feature:
  The Ark was created at God´s command and according to God's instructions

The Ark is Carried into the Temple
Limburg brothers, ca. 1410–1416, from the Very Rich Hours of the Duke de Berry, Chantilly, Musée Condé

In this book of hours*, magnificently illustrated for the Duke de Berry by Jan, Paul, and Herman Limburg, the Ark of the Covenant shimmers in gold.

Moses' Ark of the Covenant

The Ark of the Covenant is one of the most prized objects in human history. But it has been missing for over 2,500 years.

The missing object is a chest more than 3,000 years old, made of acacia wood and plated inside and outside with pure gold. Its massive golden cover contained two winged figures, divine beings who were part human and part beast—or at least this is how it's described in the Bible's Old Testament. There it is written how God commanded Moses to make the Ark of the Covenant according to God's specifications. The Ark was meant to contain the stone tablets on which God had inscribed the Ten Commandments*, the laws that God wanted all people to follow.

The Bible tells how the Israelites had long been forced to live in Egypt as slaves and servants. Then God chose Moses to lead them to a land where they could live in freedom. The Israelites took the Ark with them during their exodus from Egypt, and they kept it in a folding tent called a tabernacle. The Ark may have arrived in Jerusalem around 1000 B.C. There it is said to have stood for hundreds of years in the magnificent temple built by Israel's King Solomon.

Around 586 B.C. something terrible happened: The troops of the Babylonian king Nebuchadnezzar II looted the temple, destroyed it, and burnt all of Jerusalem

4

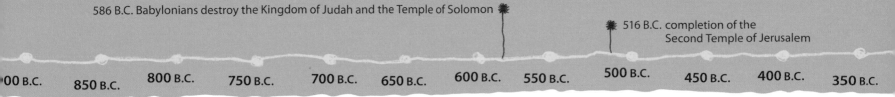

586 B.C. Babylonians destroy the Kingdom of Judah and the Temple of Solomon

516 B.C. completion of the
Second Temple of Jerusalem

00 B.C. 850 B.C. 800 B.C. 750 B.C. 700 B.C. 650 B.C. 600 B.C. 550 B.C. 500 B.C. 450 B.C. 400 B.C. 350 B.C.

Passage through the Jordan
Raphael, 1483–1520, Rome, Vatican loggia

The Ark is believed to possess tremendous power. When the Israelites had to cross the River
Jordan on their way to Jericho (in what is now Israel), the Ark supposedly held back the water
so that the Israelites could walk across on dry ground.

Aaron Places a Vessel with Manna in the Ark
Nicholas of Verdun, 1181, detail of the Verdun Altar, Klosterneuburg, parish church

The altarpiece made by French goldsmith Nicholas of Verdun is just as golden as the Ark itself. The altarpiece shows scenes from the Old* and New Testaments*.

to the ground. The Babylonians kept lists of everything they stole at that time, but the Ark is not mentioned in the lists. Could it have been destroyed? In any case, the last time the Ark is mentioned in the Bible is before the Babylonian attack.

Jews and Christians, archaeologists* and amateur researchers, scholars of religion, and adventurers would give a great deal to discover the Ark of the Covenant. Underground passages, caves, and mountains have been searched. Many suspect that the Ark is in Jordan; others think it is in the caves of Qumran in Israel. Could it have been discovered in Jerusalem 900 years ago by the Crusaders* and sent to the Pope in Rome? Or is it still in Jerusalem, possibly buried near where Solomon's Temple once stood? Today a Muslim mosque called the Dome of the Rock stands on the Temple Mount. Excavations are strictly forbidden there. In 1911 the English aristocrat, the Earl of Morley, supposedly bribed a Muslim clerk to lock him in the Dome of the Rock. He wanted to excavate secretly at night. But he was discovered before he had gotten far enough.

No one knows whether the Ark still exists or where it could be. In fact, it is not even certain that it ever existed!

Good to know
In the film Raiders of the Lost Ark by Steven Spielberg, Harrison Ford plays an archaeologist, Indiana Jones, who searches for the Ark.

David's Dance before the Ark
ca.1450, detail of the choir stall, Maulbronn, abbey

The Ark is often shown in Christian images, since the Jewish God is the same as the Christian God. Christians believe that God sent his son Jesus Christ to Earth to help humankind.

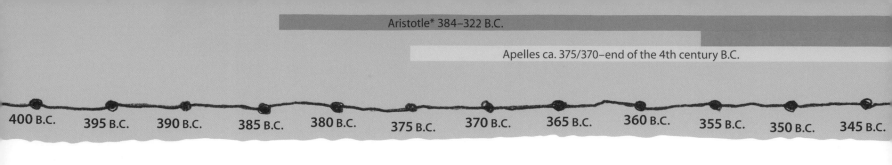

Aristotle* 384–322 B.C.

Apelles ca. 375/370–end of the 4th century B.C.

400 B.C. 395 B.C. 390 B.C. 385 B.C. 380 B.C. 375 B.C. 370 B.C. 365 B.C. 360 B.C. 355 B.C. 350 B.C. 345 B.C.

Mystery:
What did Apelles' pictures look like?

Artist:
Apelles

Date of birth and death:
ca. 375/370–end of 300s B.C.

Location:
Greece

Distinguishing feature:
Even 1,500 years after his death, Apelles remained a role model for many other painters.

Quiz question:
Did you see the donkey ears of the king? What could that mean?
(answer on p. 46)

The Riddle of Apelles

The Greek artist Apelles was the most important painter of Antiquity*. For hundreds of years, writers praised the perfection of his pictures. Yet not a single one of them has survived.

In order to get some idea of what Apelles' paintings looked like, modern people have had to rely on surviving descriptions of them. Long after his death, the artist's fame continued to intrigue many great painters. They made pictures that showed stories from Apelles' life, or they imagined for themselves—with brush and paint—how his original paintings might have looked. During the Renaissance*, when European artists rediscovered many ancient artworks, Apelles became a shining example for painters.

In the picture to the right, the Renaissance painter Botticelli imagines how Apelles' famous painting Calumny might have looked. Botticelli based his work on a surviving description by the ancient Roman writer Lucian. According to him, the two women whispering to the judging king—shown with donkey's ears as a sign of foolishness—stand for Ignorance and Mistrust. Pale-skinned Envy approaches the throne dressed in a tattered, hooded cloak; accompanied by Passion, Deceit, and Calumny, or Slander*. Calumny is dragging by the hair a sad young man: persecuted Innocence. To the left we can recognize tearful Repentance and naked Truth. Whether Lucian actually saw this painting remains just as much a mystery as the real appearance of the picture itself.

Apelles' character was just as admired as his art. Despite his great success and fame, Apelles supposedly remained modest and was never jealous of other artists.

Alexander the Great 356–323 B.C.

🌿 300 B.C. founding of Nice
by the Greek colony of Marseille

🌿 332–331 B.C. Alexander the Great conquers Egypt
🌿 331–330 B.C. Alexander conquers Persia

🌿 305 B.C. the Greek Ptolemy (one of Alexander's generals)
becomes king of Egypt

| 340 B.C. | 335 B.C. | 330 B.C. | 325 B.C. | 320 B.C. | 315 B.C. | 310 B.C. | 305 B.C. | 300 B.C. | 295 B.C. | 290 B.C. | 285 B.C. |

An art game for two or more players: Player one chooses a picture from an art book, but the other players are not allowed to see it. Player one then describes the picture as precisely as possible with words, and the other players use that description to draw or paint their own pictures. When they're finished, the players can compare their finished pictures with the original.

The Calumny of Apelles
Sandro Botticelli, ca. 1491–1495, Florence, Uffizi

Lucian writes of how Apelles based this painting on an actual experience. His envious fellow artist Antiphilus went to the Egyptian king Ptolemy and accused the artist of conspiracy against the king. Apelles would have been executed if one of the real conspirators had not confessed to the crime.

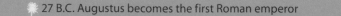

Jesus of Nazareth ca. 4 B.C.–30/31 A.D.

27 B.C. Augustus becomes the first Roman emperor

26–36 Pontius Pilate rules Judea, the province of the Roman Empire in which Jesus was born

30 B.C. 25 B.C. 20 B.C. 15 B.C. 10 B.C. 5 B.C. 0 5 A.D. 10 A.D. 15 A.D. 20 A.D. 25 A.D.

Half-length Image of Christ
6th century, Mount Sinai, Saint
Catherine's Monastery

This icon* was painted over
1,400 years ago. In the Eastern
Orhtodox church, icons are
considered more than mere
portrayals of Jesus Christ or
a saint. They are—even today—
worshipped as holy images,
in which the divine nature
of God reveals itself.

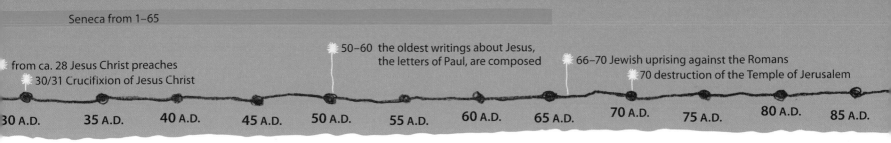
Seneca from 1–65

50–60 the oldest writings about Jesus,
the letters of Paul, are composed

from ca. 28 Jesus Christ preaches

30/31 Crucifixion of Jesus Christ

66–70 Jewish uprising against the Romans

70 destruction of the Temple of Jerusalem

30 A.D. 35 A.D. 40 A.D. 45 A.D. 50 A.D. 55 A.D. 60 A.D. 65 A.D. 70 A.D. 75 A.D. 80 A.D. 85 A.D.

What Did Jesus Really Look Like?

Most Christians imagine him as a bearded young man with long, brown hair and a thin, pale face.

Unfortunately, no portrait of Jesus painted during his lifetime has survived. Maybe he shaved regularly and had a more muscular body. Jesus was probably tan; he did live in Israel after all, where the climate is warm and sunny. Many people even doubt whether the Jesus Christ found in the Bible even existed. Christians believe that he was born as the Son of God around 2,000 years ago.

From the middle of the tenth century, more than 1,000 years ago, a special treasure was kept in the palace chapel at Constantinople (present-day Istanbul, Turkey). It was a "true portrait" of Christ, painted on a cloth. King Apgar of Edessa, who lived in what is now Urfa, Turkey, supposedly sent a messenger to have a portrait made of the living Jesus. But the artist was not able to depict Jesus as he really looked. So, as the story goes, Jesus took the cloth and pressed his face into it; leaving an impression of his face that could be seen on the cloth. This portrait, along with a letter written by Jesus, were sent to King Apgar. The "true portrait" was supposedly able to work miracles and was copied countless times. Sadly, it has been missing ever since the Crusaders attacked Constantinople in 1204 A.D.

Meanwhile, in the Church of Saint Peter in Rome, there was another, very similar impression of Jesus' face. According to legend, it was made while Jesus was carrying the cross on which he would be crucified*. A woman standing along

Mystery:
What did Jesus really look like?
Dates:
ca. 4 B.C.– 30/31 A.D.
Location:
Israel
Distinguishing feature:
As legend has it, some images of Jesus Christ were created from a "self-portrait" by Jesus himself, who made an impression of his own face in a cloth.

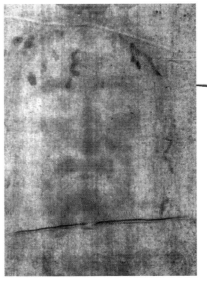

Shroud of Turin, detail with impression of a head
Turin Cathedral

On the fabric of the shroud, many traces of wounds can be seen in the area of the face. Did this man wear a crown of thorns*? Jesus Christ was called King of the Jews by many of his followers. At the end of his life, Jesus was arrested and given a thorny "crown" by his soldier guards..

Saint Veronica displays
the sudarium (or sweat
cloth) of Jesus Christ,
upon which he made
an impression of his face
on the road to his death.
In the background is
the "heavenly" Jerusalem;
this is how heaven was
thought to look.

the way handed him a cloth to dry his sweat and wipe away the blood.
Jesus then made an impression of his face in the cloth. The woman's name
was Veronica, derived from the Latin words "vera icon," meaning"
true image." The portrait disappeared in 1527, when Rome was attacked
by German and Spanish soldiers.

In the cathedral of Saint John the Baptist in Turin, Italy, a myserious linen
cloth has been kept since 1578 and only rarely shown to visitors. On the cloth,
the indistinct body of a bearded man with a thin face can be made out.

Saint Luke Painting the Virgin Mary
Derick Baegert,
ca. 1485, Münster,
LWL-Landesmuseum
fuer Kunst- und
Kulturgeschichte

Saint Luke was not only one of the evangelists*, he was also believed to have been a painter. Many images show him painting a portrait of the Christ child with his mother, Mary. Derick Baegert has relocated this scene from the Holy Land to the Europe of his own day, the 1400s. Look closely, and you'll see a medieval town through the window. Can you find the angel in the adjoining room, mixing paint for Luke? And what is the ox doing there? The ox is a symbol of the evangelist, and it is often shown together with Luke or, symbolically, in place of him.

Stigmata (or wounds) and traces of blood indicate that the person had been crucified. Many faithful Christians believe the cloth in Turin to be the shroud of Jesus Christ, in which he was wrapped after his death on the cross and In whIch he was burled. But a scientific dating of the fabric has shown that the cloth is not 2,000 years old, but only about 700 or 800. It is also unclear whether the image is even an impression at all. Perhaps it is a very clever painting technique? Numerous investigations have come up with different answers. The Catholic church considers the cloth not a relic*, but an icon. What Jesus Christ really looked like will continue to be a mystery.

The Arnolfini Portrait
Jan van Eyck, 1434,
London, National Gallery

Look at the coat Giovanni
Arnolfini is wearing in
van Eyck's portrait! With
oil paints the artist was
able to make even the
fine fur trim look realistic.

Quiz question:
Who can be seen
in the mirror?
(answer on p. 46)

Jan van Eyck and Oil Painting

Artists once had to make their paints themselves.
Each painter had his or her own recipe.
The Flemish painter Jan van Eyck often used oil paint.

Mystery:
Who invented oil painting?
Artist:
Jan van Eyck
Work:
The Arnolfini Portrait
Date:
1434
Location:
Bruges (Belgium)

Artist's colors appear red, yellow, or blue because of the tiny pigments, or particles of color, that they contain. The word "pigment" is derived from the Latin pigmentum and means "paint" or "make-up." Pigments can be made from plants, animals, soil, or minerals. The madder plant, for example, produces a deep red known as madder lake. Precious shades of red are obtained from the cochineal insect and from the murex sea snail. Lapis lazuli, a semiprecious stone, can be ground into fine powder for making ultramarine blue.

To be able to paint with these tiny colored particles so that they stick to the painted surface, a binder is needed. In the Middle Ages, many binders were made from eggs and then mixed with plant oil and water to produce tempera paint. Gouache* paints were bound in the Middle Ages with animal or plant-based glue. Both of these kinds of paints dried quickly and could be easily used and reused by the painter.

For oil paints, the pigments are bound with seed or nut oil and then mixed with turpentine*. This kind of paint dries very slowly. But the painter can apply it in many transparent (see-through) layers, or glazes, on the painting's surface. By doing this, the artist can create colors that are very shiny and deep—or produce subtle changes of color from a dark shade to a light shade. Jan van Eyck's skill as a painter was so great that he was long thought to be the inventor of oil painting. But this is unlikely. Oil paints were probably known long before van Eyck.

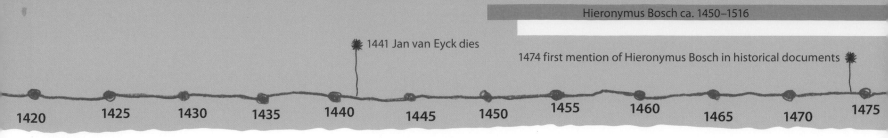

The Garden of Earthly Delights, detail of central panel
Hieronymus Bosch, 1480–1490, Madrid, Prado

Should we be afraid of these birds? Or can we trust them? One man, with his head in a glass bubble, is riding one of the feathered friends. But who are the fearful and astonished looking people to the left near the goose?

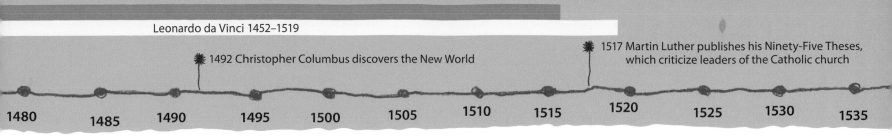
The World of Hieronymus Bosch

Hieronymus Bosch was a painter with many secrets. His real name was Jheronimus Anthonissen van Aken. But he named himself after his hometown of 's-Hertogenbosch. Strange and fantastical creatures can be seen in his images; creatures unlike those of any other artist.

Mystery:
  What is the meaning of Hieronymus Bosch´s strange creatures?
Artist:
  Hieronymus Bosch
Work:
  The Garden of Earthly Delights
Date:
  1480–1490
Location:
  's-Hertogenbosch (Netherlands)

The most puzzling of his paintings is The Garden of Earthly Delights. This title did not come from the artist himself; we don't know what he called the work. The painting was created on three wooden panels: a large one in the middle and two thinner ones to the left and right, which could be folded open or shut. This three-part holy painting (or alter) is called a triptych, from the Greek for "three" (tri) and "folding panel" (ptychon). Many altarpieces in Bosch's lifetime were triptychs. They showed scenes from the Bible, and artists had to paint them according to very specific rules. Bosch often did not follow these visual rules. This is why his works are so puzzling to scholars.

The back sides of The Garden of Earthly Delights are also painted. But here there are no bright colors—only black, white, and gray. At the time it was common to decorate the outsides of folding altarpieces with such "grisaille" paintings, which could be seen when the wings were closed. Only on Sundays and feast days* were the wings opened to show the colorfully painted insides to people who worshipped at the church. Bosch painted a very unusual picture on the outside: an enormous, transparent bubble on a dark background, surrounded by nothingness. God sits enthroned in the upper left corner, holding a book in his hand: the Bible, perhaps? The Bible is the source of the Latin verses that the painter has written along the top of the two panels: "Ipse dixit et facta sunt" and "Ipse mandavit et creata sunt."

Who is this woman with
an apple in her hand
behind a glass with nobs
on it? Is it Eve? And the
man beside her? Perhaps
the painter himself?

Not everyone believes in
a paradise in the afterlife.
But everyone has his or
her own idea of a paradise
on Earth. Can you paint your
own earthly paradise?

Translated, these verses mean: "For he spoke and it came
to be" and "he commanded and it stood forth." But wait!
Aren't the pages of the book empty? Many scholars
believe that this somber image depicts the world
after the Great Flood, which, according to the
Biblical account, was sent by God to punish people
for their sins. Others believe it is an image of the
world on the third day of creation: On the third day,
God separated the land from the waters and created
plants. But there was no light yet, and so neither were
there colors. Animals and people would be created by
God on the fifth and sixth days, according to Biblical tradition.

But what a blaze of colors can be seen when the triptych's panels are
opened! On the left side panel Bosch paints the first humans, Adam and
Eve, in paradise. On the large central panel humans and animals romp
around together. Some of the animals exist in nature, while others are
imaginary creatures invented by the artist. Are the people in some kind of
"Land of Cockaigne," where birds feed them fruit? Or are they abandoning
themselves to idleness and thinking only of their pleasure, for which God
will punish them in hell. Art scholars have different opinions as to the
meaning of this work. In his depiction of hell on the right side panel, Bosch
has used all the powers of his imagination and invented terrifying monsters.
They torture humans as punishment for evil deeds. Terrible images like this
were supposed to teach the faithful to be afraid and to illustrate for them
what they could expect after death if they did not follow God's law and
the rules of the church.

The puzzles in Bosch's paintings and his unusual depictions of paradise,
heaven, and hell led many church leaders to dislike the picture. But these
opinions did not diminish the artist's fame in the least.

The Garden of Earthly Delights, Detail of the left wing
Hieronymus Bosch, 1480–1490, Madrid, Prado

On the left side panel there is a fountain in the center that, according to the Bible, "watered the whole face of the ground". Bosch's amazing pink creation looks almost like a man-eating plant. Which animals can you find here? What kind of a strange two-legged dog is that near the giraffe? Not everything here is peaceful and happy. Look carefully! What doesn't fit? Why might Hieronymus Bosch have added scenes that don't fit in the picture at all?

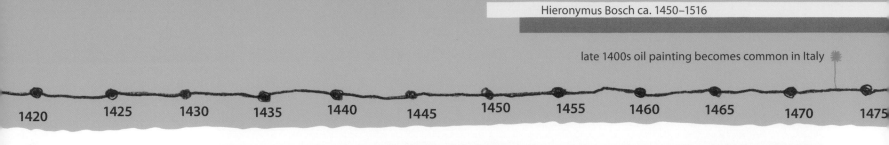

late 1400s oil painting becomes common in Italy

1420 1425 1430 1435 1440 1445 1450 1455 1460 1465 1470 1475

Mona Lisa

Leonardo da Vinci,
1503–1506, Paris, Louvre

The Mona Lisa can be
seen in the Louvre in
Paris, but only behind
bullet-proof glass.
Visitors swarm before
the portrait. Everyone
wants to admire her
famous smile!

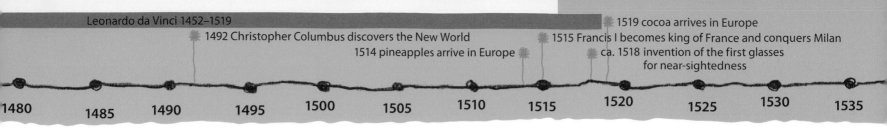

Leonardo da Vinci 1452–1519
1492 Christopher Columbus discovers the New World
1514 pineapples arrive in Europe
1519 cocoa arrives in Europe
1515 Francis I becomes king of France and conquers Milan
ca. 1518 invention of the first glasses
for near-sightedness

1480   1485   1490   1495   1500   1505   1510   1515   1520   1525   1530   1535

Why Is Mona Lisa Smiling?

This question has been asked countless times by museum visitors, art historians, and even doctors. Scarcely any other picture has been examined as closely as this one.

The Mona Lisa is one of the most famous images in the world. Her enchanting smile has been praised in poetry and celebrated in song. Yet no one knows for certain who this mysterious woman actually was. Most art historians believe she was a lady in Florence, Italy, named Lisa Gherardi. For this reason, the painting is also called "La Gioconda."

Some doctors explain that "Mona Lisa" smiles strangely because her face was partly paralyzed, and she could not move her mouth properly. Others believe the woman no longer had any front teeth; apparently many people without front teeth smile just like this. Or is she smiling because she is pregnant or has just had a child? In 2006, Canadian scientists studied the portrait with a special technique that enabled them to see underneath the painting's surface. They discovered a transparent veil painted around the dress. Wraps like this were once worn by pregnant women and new mothers.

But is the woman in the painting really smiling? The American psychologist* Margaret Livingstone believes that her smile is visible only when the viewer looks at her eyes. If you look at her mouth, Livingstone claims, her facial expression appears bland. But other people hold the opposite opinion: Only the mouth makes her face seem to smile. You can decide for yourself by covering over first Mona Lisa's mouth and then her eyes with a sheet of paper. Which feature most clearly gives Mona Lisa her famous look?

Mystery:
Why is Mona Lisa smiling?
Artist:
Leonardo da Vinci
Work:
Mona Lisa
Date:
1503–1506
Location:
Florence (Italy)

Tip
Visit http://www.citesci-ences.fr/francais/ala_cite/expo/explora/image/mona/en.php to change the expression of "Mona Lisa" with a click of the mouse.

Michelangelo Merisi da Caravaggio 1571–1610

1565 Siege of Malta by the Turks

1541 the Spanish conquer the Mayan Empire
in the Yucatan (Mexico)

1566 founding of Valletta, the modern capital of Malta

1568 first written mention
of a camera obscura with lens

1550 Naples is the largest city in Italy

1535   1540   1545   1550   1555   1560   1565   1570   1575   1580   1585   1590

How Did Caravaggio Die?

The painter Caravaggio led a wild life. In 1603, he slew
an opponent after playing a ball game in Rome.
He was then forced to flee the city and would never return.

Mystery:
  How did
  Caravaggio die?
Artist:
  Michelangelo Merisi
  da Caravaggio
Was alive from:
  1571–1610
Lived in:
  Italy, Malta

Insulting people, drinking too much, getting into fights: examples of his
bad behavior were many. Caravaggio had a quick temper, and he could act
in cruel ways. This fiery personality can be seen in the artist's famous
paintings. There he depicted events from the Bible and from ancient
mythology*, and he depicted them so impressively and realistically
that it seemed as if they had just taken place nearby. Caravaggio made
these events particularly exciting by using a painting technique called
"chiaroscuro"—striking contrasts of light and dark shades—for which he is
still famous today.

Bacchus
Caravaggio, ca. 1597,
Florence, Uffizi

Caravaggio also knew
how to enjoy life. Doesn't
Bacchus* here look like
he's inviting the viewer to
drink a toast with him?

Caravaggio produced much of his best work
in Rome. But when he was forced to flee the
city after being convicted of murder, he was
given a friendly welcome on the island of
Malta in 1607. He was a knight of the Order
of Malta* and was allowed to work on the
island as a painter. One of the works he
painted there can still be seen in the Basilica
of Saint John the Baptist in Valletta, Malta's
capital city. But it was not long before
Caravaggio was arrested again. He had taken
part in a riot and injured a knight. But the artist
was able to escape from prison and flee to the
nearby island of Sicily in 1608. From there he made his way to Naples, a city
south of Rome, where he was attacked and seriously injured in the face.

Medusa
Caravaggio, ca. 1598,
Florence, Uffizi

Caravaggio was able,
like few other painters,
to represent violence,
fear, and horror in his
images. Here he shows
the hideous snake-headed
Medusa*, and she's
realistic enough to give
the viewer a good scare!

He died in 1610, just before his thirty-ninth birthday, and his remains were
probably buried in a small Italian town called Porto Ercole.

Exactly how Caravaggio's died is still a mystery, even today. Some believe on
the basis of records that he died in a hospital from malaria, a disease that causes terrible fevers. Others believe that he died of wounds from the attack in
Naples; an attack carried out by assassins, or paid killers. After all, Caravaggio
had an often violent nature, and he had made many enemies.

The Art of Painting
Jan Vermeer, ca.
1666–1667, Vienna,
Kunsthistorisches Museum

Vermeer creates a realistic
space in this painting.
The heavy, patterned,
rug-like curtain to the left
and the chair below it
lead the viewer's eye into
the room. Our attention
is thus directed to the
woman in her blue
gown, just as the artist
himself concentrates on
this model.

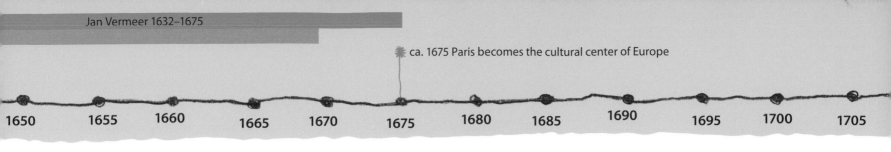

Was Jan Vermeer a Photographer?

In The Art of Painting, Dutch artist Jan Vermeer invites the viewer into his studio in Delft. But did the artist use only brushes, paint, canvas, and an easel to make his pictures?

Artists and scholars have long suspected that Vermeer might have used a camera obscura when designing his compositions. The term "camera obscura" is Latin for "dark chamber," and it was used to produce a realistic image of something. The cameras that we use today for taking photographs were created, in part, from ideas invented for the camera obscura. Camera obscuras were known well before Vermeer's time. People in ancient China mentioned them as far back as 2,500 years ago!

The Dutch scientist Christiaan Huygens, who lived in Holland at the same time as Vermeer, improved the camera obscura by using lenses that sharpened the images produced by the device. Vermeer may have had a camera like the one Huygens developed, but there are no records of him owning one. It is the design of Vermeer's own paintings that make scholars think he used a camera obscura.

Perhaps you have noticed that a tall person, when seen from afar, appears much shorter than a short person standing in front of you. The brain compensates for this difference in size between close and distant objects, so that in everyday life we often are not aware of it. But the difference can be seen clearly in a photograph and in the images produced by a camera obscura. And in Vermeer's The Art of Painting, the model with the laurel wreath seems to stand farther away from the viewer than does the seated artist, since she is depicted as being much smaller than the artist. Did Vermeer understand the tricks of photography before the invention of the photograph?

Mystery:
  Did Jan Vermeer paint his picture with the help of a camera obscura?
Artist:
  Jan Vermeer
Work:
  The Art of Painting
Date:
  1666–1667
Location:
  Delft (Netherlands)

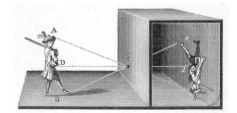

Camera Obscura
After Louis-Jacques Goussier, 1767, illustration from the Encyclopedia of Denis Diderot

An entire room or a container can serve as a camera obscura. The interior should be black except for the light-colored rear wall. On the front is a small hole. In keeping with the laws of optics (what the eye sees), the light rays entering the hole shine an upside-down, "mirror" image upon the rear wall.

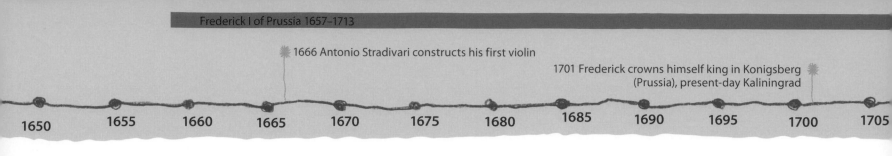

The Amber Room
Andreas Schluter, et al, 1701–1711,
Pushkin, Catherine Palace (copy from 1979–2003)

Art historians, restorers, and artisans performed an almost
unbelievable feat when they had the Amber Room reproduced
true to the original. Now it sparkles just as it did before.

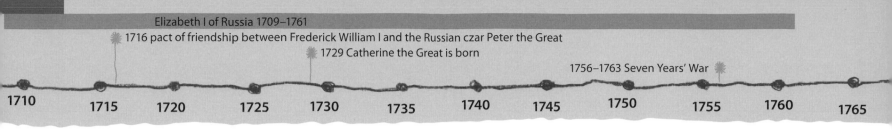
The Missing Amber Room

How it sparkles and shines! But the Amber Room that we see today in the Catherine Palace is only a copy. The location of the original room has not been known for over sixty-five years.

The precious wall panels were commissioned by Frederick I, the first king of the German state of Prussia. His court sculptor Andreas Schluter designed the room, and master craftsmen created the amber decoration between 1701 and 1711. Frederick I probably did not live to see the room completed. His son, Frederick William I, who was not very interested in art or magnificent display, gave the room as a gift to Russian Tsar Peter the Great in 1716. Peter's daughter, Tsarina Elizabeth I, had the room built into the Catherine Palace, not far from Saint Petersburg, in 1755. Her successor, Catherine the Great, selected it as her favorite room.

At the time, amber was coveted by European royal families and their courts. Jewelry, figures, and valuable objects were carved out of amber. Frederick I had lots of the material in his kingdom; it would wash up on the shores of the Baltic Sea by the ton. The pieces were gathered on the beach or fished from the water with long nets attached to poles. Even today there are rich deposits of amber on the Baltic coast.

Mystery:
  Where is the
  Amber Room hidden?
Patron:
  Friedrich I
  of Prussia
Design:
  Andreas Schluter
Builders:
  Gottfried Wolffram,
  Ernst Schacht,
  Gottfried Turau
Work:
  The Amber Room
Date of construction:
  1701-1711
Location:
  Berlin,
  Pushkin (near
  St. Petersburg, Russia),
  Konigsberg (Prussia)/
  Kaliningrad (Russia)

Catherine Palace
Bartolomeo Francesco Rastrelli,
1749–1756, Pushkin

The blue, white, and gold
Catherine Palace is a worthy
site for the magnificent
Amber Room. This is where
the reconstruction can
be found today.

The Amber Room
Detail of the paneling
made of amber,
Andreas Schlueter,
et al, 1701–1711,
Pushkin,
Catherine Palace
(copy from 1979–2003)

This artful carving
combines amber of
different colors. Amber
comes in various shades
of yellow, red, and brown.

The Amber Room remained in Russia for 200 years. During the Second World War, in the autumn of 1941, German armed forces brought it to Konigsberg in northern Germany. There it was held for safekeeping in the castle. In August of 1944, British and American bombers burned Konigsberg to the ground. The castle was destroyed as well. When the Soviet army occupied the town after a hard-fought battle, the precious panels had disappeared.

Amber is made when a liquid called resin, which comes from trees, fossilizes (hardens) over millions of years. About forty to fifty-four million years ago, an enormous "amber forest" covered Northern Europe. Scientists believe this giant forest was flooded by the sea, and the ocean washed the already hardened pine resin onto land. There it was covered by soil and, over the course of many millions of years, compressed into amber. During the Ice Age, about 20,000 years ago, huge sheets of ice called glaciers partially eroded (or wore down) the soil on top of the amber. These glaciers eventually melted and washed the amber into the North Sea and the Baltic. From there it has been washing up onto the shores of Denmark, Poland, and Lithuania for as long as anyone can remember.

Tip

Here's how you can test whether amber is real or not: Rub the material vigorously against some wool and then hold a small scrap of paper against it. If the scrap of paper sticks to the material, then it is real amber. Amber behaves in this way because of a phenomenon called static electricity*. In fact, the word electricity is derived from "electron," the ancient Greek word for amber. The first observations of electricity were made with amber. You can also place the amber in a glass of fresh water and then in a glass of saltwater. The amber sinks to the bottom of the fresh water, but it floats in the saltwater.

Ever since that time, people have sought to find the remains of the Amber Room. Are they still hidden in Konigsberg, maybe in the dark tunnels underneath where the castle once stood? Or were they removed from Konigsberg in the nick of time and hidden somewhere else? Maybe they're in a mine in the Erz Mountains of Germany? So far no trace of the panels has been found. But old photographs have turned up, and with their help experts were able to reconstruct the room between 1979 and 2003. This project used a total of six tons of amber!

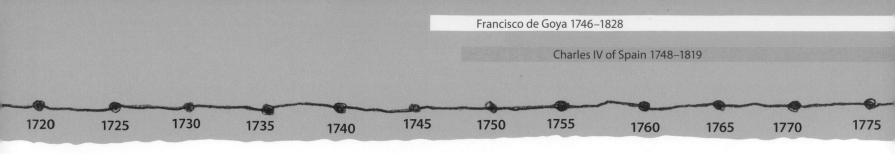

The Family of Charles IV
Francisco de Goya,
1800–1801, Madrid, Prado

This family portrait
shows 14 members
of the royal family -
and the painter himself.

Queen María Luisa 1751–1819

1788 Charles IV becomes king
1789 start of the French Revolution
1808 Charles IV is forced to give up his throne

1780   1785   1790   1795   1800   1805   1810   1815   1820   1825   1830   1835

Goya and the Ugly Queen

In 1800 Francisco de Goya created a puzzling portrait of the Spanish royal family. Do these people look like royalty? If not for their splendid clothing, they could be the family next door!

Mystery:
Did the court painter Goya want to make fun of the Spanish royal family?
Artist:
Francisco Jose de Goya y Lucientes
Work:
The Family of Charles IV
Date: 1800–1801
Location:
Madrid (Spain)

Charles IV and his wife commissioned a family portrait from their court painter Goya. Even in the 1800s the painting was considered strange. A French art critic laughed at the painting, saying that the Spanish royal couple looked like a baker and his wife who had just won the lottery. Many other art experts think that the royal family was shown in an unflattering way. Did Goya want to secretly mock the family with this picture?

Charles IV was not considered very intelligent. He was said to enjoy hunting more than his duties as king. Of the queen it was whispered that she constantly had new lovers. She and her lover Manuel de Godoy were considered to be the real rulers of Spain. In fact, royal families in general were not viewed very well by Europeans at the end of the 1700s. In 1789 the French Revolution broke out. The French king and queen were deposed, and in 1793 they were executed. In his art, Goya increasingly showed that people needed to be free of war and bad governments. In 1824 he left Spain to live in France, where there was more freedom for artists. Is it possible to see Goya's critical attitude of Spain in his picture of the royal family?

Not all art critics agree. Some believe that the painting is a family portrait that follows all the expected rules: The focus of the painting is the royal couple, who draw the viewer's eye upon themselves. All the other family members are grouped around them. In keeping with his status, the king stands with his foot forward, one step in front of the queen, who can be found exactly in the center of the image.

A large family! Charles IV and Maria Luisa had fourteen children, but six of them died in childhood. Just to the right of the picture's center stands the head of the family, King Charles IV (fifty-two years old). Near him to the left is Queen Maria Luisa (forty-nine). Between the King and Queen, holding his mother's hand, is the youngest son, Infant Don Francisco de Paula (six). The queen's right arm is around her daughter Dona Maria Isabel (eleven). Next to the queen, from left to right, are: son Don Carlos Maria Isidoro (twelve); Don Ferdinand, Prince of Asturias (sixteen), the eldest son and heir to the throne; the king's sister, Dona Maria Josefa; and the Princess Maria Amalia. Goya painted Maria Amalia with her face in shadow and turned away from the viewer, for she had already died in 1798 at the age of nineteen. On the other side of the picture, to the right of the king, stands (from left to right): the king's brother, Don Antonio Pascual; the king's eldest daughter, Dona Carlota Joaquina, Princess of Portugal and Brazil (twenty-five); the king's son-in-law, Don Luis de Borbon, Prince of Parma (twenty-seven); and Luis' wife, Dona Maria

Luisa Josefina (eighteen), with their little son, Carlos Luis. Have you also found the artist? You can make him out in the background on the left, next to his easel.

All the male family members wear the sash of the Order of Charles III, the father of Charles IV; all the female members wear the sash of the Order of Queen Maria Luisa.

Francisco Jose de Goya y Lucientes—this was his full name— depicts himself as proud and serious-looking in this work, which shows his paints and painting hat. Goya could attach a candle onto the painting hat when he worked at night.

Maybe, in fact, Goya painted the women of the family to look better than they did in real life? Princess Carlota Joaquina was reported to have been short and ugly. She was said to have been cross-eyed with a swollen red nose, black and greenish-yellow teeth, and skin full of acne. None of that can be seen here, because the painter has cleverly hidden the princess behind her brother-in-law on the right side of the picture. Nor was the queen known at court for her beauty. Her many pregnancies and illnesses had ruined her body. A Russian diplomat at the time said, "Her skin is greenish and the loss of almost all her teeth, which have been replaced by false ones, finished off what was left of her looks." In the family portrait, a flattering light surrounds the women. Did Goya paint Queen Maria Luisa prettier than she actually was?

What do you think? Did Goya create a dignified picture of the Spanish royal family, or did he unmask the family's stupidity and thirst for power? We will probably never know what Goya really thought. In any case, no evidence has survived that the king and queen complained about their odd family portrait.

Quiz question:
Charles IV was the grandfather of Prince Carlos Luis. What is the relationship between Don Francisco de Paula and Carlos Luis? And what is the relationship between Carlos Luis and Dona Maria Josefa?
(answer on p. 46)

Draw or paint a portrait of your own family. Think about how you would like to arrange the family members. Where would you place yourself in the painting? Maybe near your favorite aunt?

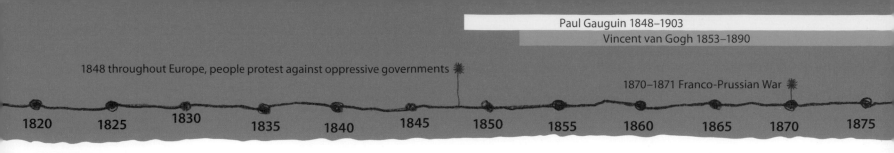

Mystery:
What exactly happened on the evening of December 23, 1888?

Artists:
Vincent van Gogh and Paul Gauguin

Evidence:
A bloody package and two self-portraits

Location:
Arles (France)

To Whom Did van Gogh Give His Ear?

"Last Sunday, around 11:30 pm, a certain Vincent van Gogh, painter, originally from Holland, entered Maison de la Tolérance No. 1, demanded to see a certain Rachel and … gave her his ear, saying, 'Take good care of this object.' Then he disappeared."

This quote came from a local newspaper in Arles, a town in southern France, on December 30, 1888. After van Gogh gave his ear away, the police were informed and brought the poor artist to a hospital on the following day.

The Painter of Sunflowers: Portrait of Vincent van Gogh
Paul Gauguin, 1888,
Amsterdam,
Van Gogh Museum

Sunflowers were van Gogh's favorite subject and he made several pictures of them.

The report describes the act of a desperate man. For nine weeks van Gogh had been living together with his painter friend Paul Gauguin in the "yellow house" in Arles. How much van Gogh had looked forward to his guest's arrival! Together with Gauguin, van Gogh had hoped to realize the dream of living an artist's life in Arles. The two friends had hoped to capture the special light of southern France and to make the colors of their paintings truly glow. But it soon became clear that van Gogh and Gaugin were too different to live and work together. Their disputes about art and life became more and more angry. And then the catastrophe: After an intense fight, van Gogh cut off his left earlobe with a razor—or was it his whole ear? In any case, the painter had lost so much blood that the hospital feared he would die.

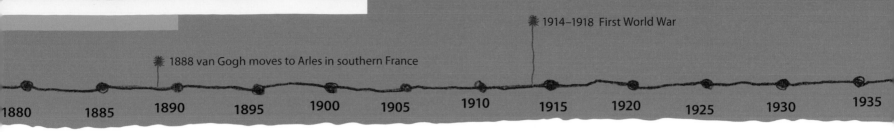

**Self-Portrait with
Bandaged Ear**
Vincent van Gogh,
1889, London, Courtauld
Institute Galleries

Vincent van Gogh just
barely survived
his self-mutilation.

Quiz question:
Why is the bandage in
van Gogh's self-portrait
on the left side?
(answer on p. 46)

Van Gogh's sister-in-law, Johanna Bonger, the wife of his brother Theo,
later wrote that van Gogh only cut off a part of his ear. In his memoirs,
Paul Gauguin claimed that van Gogh had attacked him with the razor.
But he had been able to fend his friend off with a stern look. After
rushing from the house, van Gogh cut off his ear. Other witnesses also
report that van Gogh cut off the entire ear and wrapped it in packing paper.
In any case, Gauguin did not return to the yellow house. What exactly
happened on that evening—and the identity of the woman to whom van
Gogh gave his ear—will probably never be known.

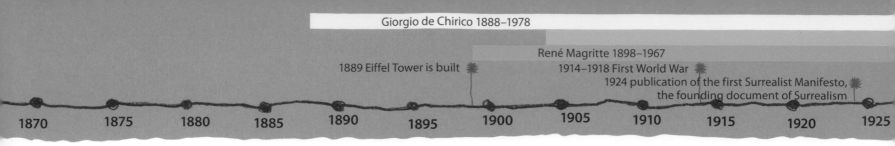

Giorgio de Chirico 1888–1978

René Magritte 1898–1967

1889 Eiffel Tower is built

1914–1918 First World War

1924 publication of the first Surrealist Manifesto, the founding document of Surrealism

1870 1875 1880 1885 1890 1895 1900 1905 1910 1915 1920 1925

Melancholy and Mystery of a Street
Giorgio de Chirico, 1914, private collection

The title of the picture Melancholy and Mystery of a Street aptly describes the strange atmosphere of de Chirico's picture.

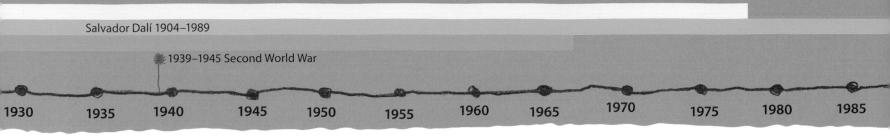
Surrealistic Picture Puzzles

Have you ever had the feeling that familiar things suddenly seem totally strange, as if you had never seen them before? Do you feel as if they were concealing some kind of secret?

Mystery:
  What is depicted in the Surrealists' paintings?
Artists:
  Giorgio de Chirico and the Surrealists
Date:
  1910s-1950s
Location:
  France, Italy, Spain

That is what happened to several painters and authors in the early 1900s. They set out to discover the strange things that await beyond everyday reality. They called their artistic movement Surrealism*.

The Italian artist Giorgio de Chirico was the great role model for the Surrealist painters. He often suffered from long illnesses, and his ill health may have led him to see the world in new ways. Ordinary towns with their streets, gardens, and squares came to seem new and very strange to him. The impression was both unsettling and fascinating at the same time. De Chirico decided to show this magical atmosphere in his pictures. To do so, he used a few tricks that can be seen in the painting to the right.

The picture Melancholy and Mystery of a Street looks like a town square in an Italian city on the sea. But something here is not quite right! The houses seem to lead the viewer in odd directions, giving the space a strange, uncomfortable feeling. A suspicious silence lies over the city.
The flag on the horizon seems to flutter playfully in the breeze. But no life is stirring in the dark windows or beneath the arcade. Is it too hot to go outside? The light is blazing. But despite this, the sky has darkened to a deep green. Perhaps it's already evening, since the shadows are so long. Why is there no one in the streets except for the girl and the giant shadow behind the block of houses on the right? Who could the person making that shadow be?

The Persistence of Memory
Salvador Dali, 1931,
New York,
Museum of Modern Art

The Spanish artist Salvador Dali is one of the most famous Surrealists, and he was always able to shock the public with his crazy ideas. He liked to write and talk about his work and about himself. Dali said that when he created his artwork, The Persistence of Memory, he first painted the background. But he then had no interesting idea for the foreground. One evening he went into his studio to look at the picture again. On the way there, as he was remembering how unbelievably soft the good Camembert cheese had been for dinner, an idea came to him. He would finish the painting with soft clocks: an image symbolizing the passage of time. But even if Dali had not given this explanation, his work would still look magical and strange.

The girl with the tire appears to be nothing but a shadow. But since when have shadows been able to cast shadows themselves? And why is the wagon in the foreground open? Is it a construction trailer or a circus wagon? Does it belong to the girl? Where do the streetcar tracks to the lower right lead? Theses are all questions raised by Giorgio de Chirico that no one can answer. The artist doesn't even want us to solve the puzzle. The picture is supposed to remain mysterious forever!

Maybe you would also like to paint or draw a "surreal" picture. You can make objects look unfamiliar by changing their size, their color, or other qualities. You can also bring things together that have nothing to do with each other. After all, clocks in real life can't really hang like cloth over the trees!

Personal Values
Rene Magritte, 1952, private collection

What happened here?
The Belgian Surrealist Rene Magritte looked with new eyes at simple objects familiar to everyone. Here, instead of wallpaper, the walls of the bedroom are covered with a brilliant cloud-filled sky. Comb, glass, soap, shaving brush, and matches are all enormous—much too big to use. In this way, the objects that we take so much for granted—objects that we often don't notice—come to seem unfamiliar and thrilling.

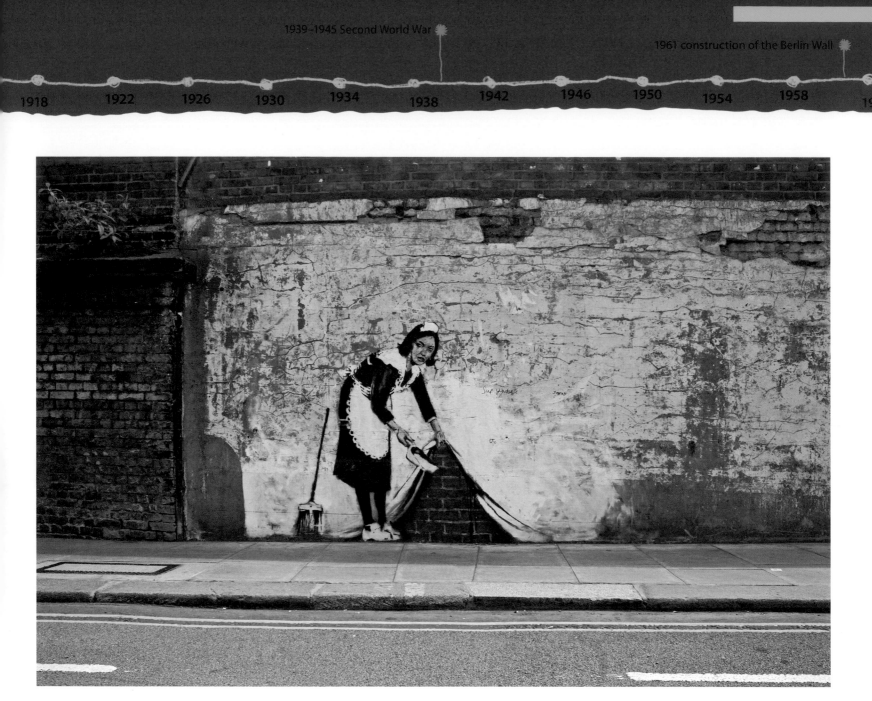

London, 2006 –
for the maid

Banksy produces his graffiti with the help
of stencils and spray paint. His technique
enables him to produce art quickly on
walls and other surfaces. Banksy can then
swiftly disappear back into the darkness
of night without being seen!

Jeff Koons is born 1955

Banksy is probably born 1974

1987 Andy Warhol dies

1989 fall of the Berlin Wall

2008 Barack Obama is elected first African-American president of the United States

1966   1970   1974   1978   1982   1986   1990   1994   1998   2002   2006   2010

Who Is Banksy?

He comes secretly in the night. He paints graffiti* on walls and the sides of houses throughout the world.
He smuggles his own images into the largest museums.
But no one has ever seen him.

Banksy was probably born in 1974 in Bristol, England. His real name might be Rob, Robin, or Robert Banks. After finishing school, Banksy is said to have trained to be a butcher. Supposedly not even his parents know that he is a famous artist. In 2008 an English newspaper claimed to have solved the mystery of Banksy's true identity. His name was Robin Gunningham, he came from an affluent family, and he had gone to an expensive private school. Yet there was no comment from Banksy, and the newspaper could not prove its story.

In 2004 a painting that Banksy had smuggled into New York City's Museum of Modern Art hung there for six days. It showed a soup can that looked like one of artist Andy Warhol's famous Campbell's Tomato Soup can paintings from the 1960s. Banksy's can, however, bore the word "Tesco," the name of a well-known British supermarket. A year later Banksy secretly placed one of his paintings in the British Museum in London. The work looked like an ancient cave painting, showing a buffalo pierced by spears. But the picture also showed a very modern image: a man with a shopping cart. Remarkably, Banksy's "fake" art remained undetected for several days!

Mystery:
Who is Banksy?
Date of birth:
Probably 1974
Birthplace:
Probably Bristol
(United Kingdom)
Occupation:
Street artist*
Has left traces in:
Australia, Germany,
Israel, Italy, Jamaica,
Cuba, Mali, Mexico,
Palestine, Spain, and
the United States
Distinguishing feature:
His actions are
against the law and,
at the same time, art

Scene from the film Exit Through the Gift Shop
Banksy, 2010

Banksy has just shot his first film, Exit Through the Gift Shop, about a director who wants to make a film about Banksy. But here too, the street artist's face is never seen and his voice is distorted.

Bethlehem, 2007 –
for the Donkey

Banksy's graffiti is not always funny. He frequently comments on social and political themes. This picture is about two peoples who live together in Israel but who have long been in conflict: the Israelis and the Palestinians.

In 2009, the Bristol Museum in England invited Banksy to create a "real" art exhibit. In this show, the artist revealed many strange creations. One of them showed sausages that had motor engines and could move on their own!

In the meantime, Banksy's works sell for high prices at auctions. But the sale of his graffiti sprayed onto walls has posed problems: The buyer also has to purchase the house on which the art is painted! In London, one graffiti by Banksy of a spray-painted rat was stolen in 2007 by simply chipping it off the wall. A few weeks later the painting was offered for sale on Ebay for 30,000 British pounds.

Banksy must avoid becoming known at any price. Otherwise he could no longer carry out secret actions. And also, not everyone values his art; if anything, some people want to put him on trial for tresspassing and property damage. Yet the mystery surrounding Banksy's identity has made him world-famous and driven up the prices of his art. So the world will probably continue to ask itself: Who is Banksy?

With the help of a stencil you can design a t-shirt yourself and make it into a unique piece of clothing. Start for example with your first name. Use an X-Acto knife (careful, you'll need a good cutting pad underneath) to cut your name's letters out of heavy paper or cardboard so that the letters fall out and the paper around them stays in place. When the stencil is finished, lay the t-shirt down flat on several sheets of newspaper or a large plastic cloth. Place your stencil over the shirt and spray over the cut-out letters with spray paint.

Glossary

ANTIQUITY The time of the ancient Greeks and Romans (ca. 800 B.C. to 500 A.D.). The term is derived from the Latin word antiquus, meaning "old."

ARCHAEOLOGISTS Experts in the study of ancient times. They search for evidence of human culture, often found through excavations.

BACCHUS The god of wine in Roman antiquity.*

BOOK OF HOURS A book for prayers and devotions to be performed at specific hours of the day. Books of hours were written in beautiful script and then decorated with precious paintings.

CROWN OF THORNS At the end of his life, Jesus was captured by soldiers of the Roman Empire, which ruled Jerusalem in Jesus' day. These soldiers didn't believe that Jesus was a real king, so they made fun of him by giving him a fake "crown" of thorny branches.

CRUCIFY To kill a person by hanging his body on a cross and leaving him to die. Jesus Christ was crucified in a particularly terrible way— his hands and feet were nailed to the cross.

CRUSADERS Christian soldiers led by kings and noblemen who, between the end of the 1000s A.D. and the end of the 1200s A.D., set off from Europe to conquer Jerusalem and the Holy Land, which were then under Muslim rule.

EVANGELIST Bringer of the "glad tidings" of the Gospels (also known as the "Evangelion"). In the New Testament the four Evangelists, Matthew, Mark, Luke, and John, tell the life of Jesus Christ.

FEAST DAY is a part of many Christian church traditions. Feast days honor particular Christian saints or martyrs who sacrificed and died for their faith.

GOUACHE Intensely colored paints that are thinned with water before they are used. The term gouache is derived from guazzo, the Italian word for "puddle of water."

GRAFFITI Paintings and drawings on the walls of buildings, bridges, or fences; mostly done with spray paint.

GREEK MYTHOLOGY The stories of the gods and heroes of ancient Greece.

ICON A religious image with the representation of Christ, the Virgin Mary, or one of the saints. An icon is not an ordinary portrait. It is believed that the divine nature of God reveals itself in an icon.

MEDUSA The female monster of Greek mythology* who had hair made of live snakes. Whoever looked at Medusa was turned to stone on the spot.

NEW TESTAMENT Dating from the time of the earliest Christians, this part of the Bible tells the story of Jesus Christ.

OLD TESTAMENT The holy writings of Judaism, also called the Tanakh. The Bible is made up of both the Old and New Testaments.

ORDER OF MALTA An organization of Christian soldiers that long defended the island of Malta, in the Mediterranean Sea, from attack by invaders.

PSYCHOLOGIST A doctor who studies the mind and how people behave.

RELIC (from the Latin reliquie for "remains") A body part of a saint or an object touched by that saint during his or her life. Relics were considered holy and often kept in precious containers.

RENAISSANCE The term is derived from the Latin rinascita, meaning "rebirth." During the Renaissance, which lasted from the first half of the 1400s to around 1600, the culture of ancient Greece and Rome was rediscovered.

SLANDER Lies that are told about people on purpose, usually to cause those people harm.

STATIC ELECTRICITY A kind of force, or energy, that builds up on the surface of an object. Static electricity often causes objects to attach to each other or to repel each other.

STREET ART Art that is created on the walls

of buildings, lampposts, traffic signs, and other surfaces. Street artists often spray paint or glue things onto these surfaces. Most street art is made illegally, which is why their creators usually like to remain anonymous.

SURREALISM An artistic movement that originated in Paris in the early 1920s. Writers and poets invented the term sur-realite, which means "beyond" the real. The Surrealists were interested in everything that went beyond reality.

TEN COMMANDMENTS Rules from the Bible that were given by God. These rules tell how people should behave toward God and toward other people.

TURPENTINE is a liquid made from the sap of trees. It is often used to produce paints.

Mixing oil paints is quite an elaborate process. But you can easily make tempera paint yourself. You'll need: One or more eggs (depending on how much paint you want to make), various colors of pigment powder from an art supply or craft store, shallow bowls or metal cups, and small plastic spoons. Mixing the paint: Separate the egg yokes from the whites; the whites you can use for baking. (Try making coconut macaroons with them!). Beat the egg yoke in a bowl. Then, using the plastic spoon, thoroughly mix equal amounts of egg yoke and pigment in the shallow bowl. The best brush to use for applying the paint is a flat bristle brush. The paint should be used as soon as possible! Try painting on the white paper of a drawing pad.

Answers to the quiz questions

page 8: The donkey ears are a sign of folly: the king is foolish because he believes the false testimony of Antiphilus and is blind to the real conspiracy against him.

page 14: The backs of the couple can be seen in the mirror, as well as two visitors who have just entered the room. Many people believe that one of these visitors might be the painter Jan van Eyck himself.

page 33: Don Francisco de Paula is the uncle of Carlos Luis, which would make Carlos Luis his nephew. Dona Maria Josefa is the great aunt of Carlos Luis.

page 35: Van Gogh probably painted his self-portrait in front of a mirror. This is why we see a mirror image of him in the picture.

The Deutsche Nationalbibliothek lists this publication in the Deutsche Nationalbibliographie; detailed bibliographic information is available at http://dnb.ddb.de.

Picture credits:
akg-images: p. 5, 6, 11 (below); ARTOTHEK: p. 13, 30; E.ON Ruhrgas AG: p. 26; James Herd, San Francisco: p. 43; Paranoid Pictures: p. 41; Pest Control Office: p. 40, 42; ullstein bild: p. 25.

Frontcover: Details taken from works by Leonardo da Vinci (p. 20), Hieronymus Bosch (p. 16), Vincent van Gogh (p. 35).
Frontispiece: Detail taken from a work by Francisco de Goya (S. 33).

Prestel Verlag, a member of Verlagsgruppe Random House GmbH
www.prestel.com

Translation: Cynthia Hall
Project coordination: Doris Kutschbach
Copy editing: Brad Finger
Editing and picture editing: Larissa Spicker
Production: Nele Krüger
Design: Michael Schmoelzl, agenten.und.freunde, Munich
Lithography: ReproLine mediateam, Munich
Printing and binding: Printer Trento, Trento

Verlagsgruppe Random House FSC-DEU-0100
The FSC-certified paper Profibulk has been supplied by Igepa, Germany.

ISBN 978-3-7913-7044-6